TOUCHSTONES VOLUME I

STUDENT'S GUIDE

Selected, Translated, and Edited by

Howard Zeiderman

Published by

TOUCHSTONES
DISCUSSION PROJECT

Fourth Edition, 2006

ISBN: 1-878461-39-7

Contents

Introduction to Touchstones

You are about to begin a class that is based on discussions. In these discussions, you will be talking to one another as well as to your teacher. We are all familiar with discussions because we have all discussed problems, feelings, opinions, and experiences with friends and relatives all our lives. However, the discussions you will have in this class will differ from your previous experiences of discussions.

Touchstones Discussions differ from your regular classes.

1. Everyone sits in a circle.
2. The teacher is a member of the group and will help, but isn't the authority who gives the correct answers.
3. There is no hand-raising; instead, everyone will learn how to run the discussion.
4. No one does homework for this class.

Touchstones Discussions differ from other discussions.

1. Discussions involve everyone in the class from your best friend to students you don't know very well.
2. Discussions are about the Touchstones Texts and not just about your own concerns and experiences.
3. Discussions will occur once a week at a scheduled time. The large group discussion will be preceded by the reading of a selected text and will begin with a question asked by the teacher or discussion leader.

Touchstones Ground Rules and Goals

Ground Rules

1. **Read the text carefully.** In Touchstones Discussions your opinions are important, but these opinions are your thoughts about the text.
2. **Listen to what others say and don't interrupt.** A discussion cannot occur if you do not listen carefully to what others say.
3. **Speak clearly.** For others to respond to your opinions, everyone must be able to hear and understand what you say.
4. **Give others your respect.** A discussion is a cooperative exchange of ideas and not an argument or a debate. You may become excited and wish to share your ideas but don't talk privately to your neighbor. In a Touchstones class, you must share your ideas with the whole class.

Goals

You will learn to—
1. listen better to what is said;
2. explain your own ideas;
3. speak and work with others whether you know them or not;
4. receive correction and criticism from others;
5. ask about what you don't understand;
6. admit when you're wrong;
7. think about questions for which the answers are uncertain;
8. teach others;
9. teach yourself;
10. become more aware of how others see you.

The Iliad: Hector and Andromache
Homer

In the 10th year of the war between the Greeks and Trojans, Agamemnon, leader of the Greeks, insulted Achilles, the Greeks' greatest warrior. While Achilles, furious, refused to fight, the Trojans led by Hector became bolder than they had ever been. For the first time in 10 years, they began fighting the Greeks away from the city. Yet, even as they won small victories, all the Trojans feared that Achilles, who had killed so many of them, would return to fight and catch them out in the open.

After one of the battles, Hector returned to the city looking for his wife, Andromache. He found her with their infant son above the city gate. They stood together holding hands and looked at their child. Hector smiled in silence but Andromache had tears in her eyes as she began to speak. "Your great courage will be what kills you. And you have no pity for me and your son. When the Greeks destroy you, it would be better if I die, too. Without you, there is nothing for me but sorrow. In one battle Achilles killed my father and seven brothers. On the day he finally released my mother for ransom, she also died. You, my husband, are now also father, mother, and brother to me. Don't make your child an orphan. Don't let your wife become a widow.

Draw your men up to the fig tree near the city. Don't go down and fight in the open spaces near the ships."

Hector, wearing his shining bronze armor, answered her. "I think about that too, woman, but how could I face my men and their wives if I stayed away from the battle? And my own spirit won't let me. Ever since I learned to fight, I've always been the best of the Trojans. I've won a great name for myself and my father. And there's one thing I know. A day will come when this city will be destroyed and my father's people will perish. And though my brothers and parents will be killed, I think about you most of all. On that day a Greek will lead you away in tears. You will be a slave in someone's home. Someday, seeing you cry, a Greek will say, 'This is the wife of Hector, greatest of the Trojans.' I pray that before I hear you crying as they take you away, I will be dead and buried in the ground."

As Hector finished, he held out his arms for his baby boy. The child screamed and pressed back harder against his nurse's bosom. His father frightened the boy, since his head was covered by a bronze helmet with a horse-hair plume like some strange animal. Hector and Andromache both laughed. The smiling warrior took off his helmet and picked up his son. He tossed him in the air and kissed him. He looked up to the sky and prayed, "Let my boy be as I am, first among the Trojans. Someday let men say of him, 'He is better by far than his father when he comes home from battle.'"

About Revenge
Francis Bacon

Revenge is a sort of savage justice. The more people try to take revenge, the more the law should punish them. When a man commits a crime, he breaks the law. But when the injured person takes revenge, the person destroys law itself. In taking revenge, a person does indeed get even with his enemy. But when one refuses to take revenge, he shows that he is better than his enemy. King Solomon, I am sure, said it is glorious for a person to forget an injury.

Whatever is past is gone and can't be changed. Wise people know they have enough to do in the present and with whatever might happen in the future. They don't spend their time taking revenge. People who spend their time worrying about past injuries just waste their time. Also, no person hurts another person just to hurt him. Rather, it is done for his profit or his own pleasure or his honor or for some other reason he might have. So why should I be angry with someone for loving himself better than he loves me? Suppose someone hurts me because he is evil. Isn't that just like a thorn or briar which scratches me because it can't do anything else?

Revenge is most allowable when there is no specific law to correct an injury. However, one must then be careful that the kind of revenge one takes does not break another law.

Some people, when they get even, want their enemy to know that it will happen. This is a more generous way of acting. Not letting your enemy know you are going to get even is a cowardly thing to do. It is like killing at night from ambush.

There was an Italian ruler, Cosimo de Medici, who said the following to his friends who might betray or injure him: "We read," he said, "that we are commanded to forgive our enemies. But we never read that we are commanded to forgive our friends." I think, however, that the spirit of what Job said is truer. He said, "Shall we receive good from God and not also be willing to accept the evil?" The same is true, in part, about friends.

What is certain about planning to get even is that one's own wounds remain open. If one didn't spend one's time trying to take revenge, those injuries would heal and be forgotten. Public or state revenges are, for the most part, good as in the case of the murderers of Julius Caesar. Private revenges are, however, not good. People who take revenge live the life of witches. They cause trouble to others and come to a bad end.

The Histories
Herodotus

Croesus, the king of Lydia, made war on all the cities in Ionia and Aeolia and conquered them. Over the next few years, he brought all the neighboring nations under his control. When all these nations became part of the Lydian empire, the wealth and strength of Sardis, the capital of Lydia, was at its greatest. At that time, some wise men from Greece visited King Croesus. One of them was Solon, from the Greek city of Athens. Croesus put Solon up in his royal palace as his guest. After a few days, the Lydian king made a point of showing his visitors the greatness of his wealth and strength. Croesus said to Solon, "You have traveled to many lands and are said to be wise. Who is the happiest man you have ever seen?" He asked this because he thought he was the happiest and wanted Solon to admit it. However, Solon answered, "Tellus of Athens, sir." Croesus was surprised and asked why. Solon said, "Because he had good handsome sons and he lived to see them all grow up. His life was comfortable. He died courageously in battle to keep his city free, and the Athenians gave him a public funeral and praised him highly."

Croesus asked a second time, "Solon, who, after Tellus, seems happiest?" expecting he would be given at least a second place. But Solon said, "Cleobis and Bito from Argos. They had all they needed and were both very good athletes. They won many prizes at the Olympic Games. They loved their mother and honored her in public. When they died, their mother and all the other women of Argos praised and honored them."

After two disappointments, Croesus spoke angrily, "Solon! Do you really believe that these common men were happier than I am?" Solon replied, "King Croesus, how can I tell if you are happy until I hear how you have died? If someone is healthy, does not have bad luck, has fine children, is good-looking, and then has a good death, he may really be called happy. But you can't call someone's life happy until it is finished. In everything we must always look at the end. Often a man is given a gleam of happiness and then ruined." These thoughts did not please Croesus. He let Solon leave, convinced that the Greek wise man was a fool.

5

The Physics: Book II, Chapter 7
Aristotle

When we see something that interests us, whether it is a natural thing or a man-made thing, we try, above all, to understand it. We don't think we really understand something until we understand why it is the way it is. Another way of saying this is that when we see something that makes us wonder, we want to know what causes it. However, it is pretty clear that the word *cause* means many different things. Let us try to list these different things and see which are the most important.

First, the material out of which something is made causes the thing to be what it is. For example, the stone out of which a statue is made causes the statue to be what it is. It would be very different if it were made out of wood.

Second, the shape or the pattern of something is also a cause of it being what it is. For example, if someone asks you how you know that a certain figure is a triangle, you will probably say that it looks like a triangle, that it has the shape of a triangle.

Third, anything that is responsible for something else is the cause of it. For example, the father and mother are causes of the baby. The sculptor causes the statue. If you ask someone for advice and when he gives it you follow it, then this person causes your action.

Fourth, cause means the goal something or someone is aiming at. This kind of cause I call the final cause because it is the most important of all the causes. If you exercise and someone asks you why, you say, "In order to be healthy." If someone asks why geese fly south every autumn, the most important answer is, "In order to get to some place warm for the winter." Finally, if someone asks why a tool, an axe, has a particular shape, the best answer is that it is shaped that way in order to cut wood.

In all these cases, the other meanings of cause also apply. For example, if someone asks why geese fly south in the autumn, other answers are that they are made out of strong muscles and light bones, or that they have wings, or that the days have grown very short and cold. All these answers are true, but the most important answer is that it is good for them to be in warm places when winter arrives. This is the final cause. It tells you what something is good for, and this is what you really want to know.

A Mathematician's Defense
Godfrey Harold Hardy

A mathematician, like a painter or a poet, is a maker of patterns. If his patterns are more permanent than theirs, it is because his are made with ideas. A painter makes patterns with shapes and colors, a poet with words. A mathematician, on the other hand, works only with ideas. So his patterns are likely to last longer, since ideas don't wear out as quickly as words.

The mathematician's patterns, like the painter's or the poet's, must be beautiful. Beauty is the first test. It may be very hard to define mathematical beauty, but that's just as true of beauty of any kind. We may not be able to say what makes a poem beautiful, but we recognize one when we read it.

A chess problem is genuine mathematics, but it is in some way "trivial" mathematics. However clever and complicated, however original and surprising the moves, there is something essential lacking. Chess problems are unimportant. The best mathematics is serious as well as beautiful—"important" if you like, but "serious" is better.

I am not thinking of the "practical" consequences of mathematics. At present, I will say only that if a chess problem is, in the crude sense "useless," then that is equally true of most of the best mathematics. Very little of mathematics is useful practically, and that little is dull. The "seriousness" of a mathematical theorem lies not in its practical consequences, which are usually slight. Instead, the seriousness of a theorem lies in the significance of the mathematical ideas it connects together. We may say, roughly, that a mathematical idea is "significant" if it can be connected in a natural way, with a large body of other mathematical ideas. By this means, the theorem is likely to lead to advances in mathematics itself, and even in the other sciences.

Leviathan
Thomas Hobbes

Nature has made men roughly equal in body and mind. When everything is considered, the difference between one man and another is not very great. The case of bodily strength serves as a good example. The weakest man has enough strength to kill the strongest. He can do this either by some trick or by using a weapon or by joining with other men. The same is true of men's minds. Inequalities can be made up for by various means.

This rough equality in ability produces in every man the equal hope of getting what he wants. So when two men desire something that only one can have, this equality encourages both to strive for it. They therefore become enemies. Each man tries to destroy or defeat the other in order to get what he needs to keep alive or to enjoy his life. If we consider what men are like when they do not live in societies, we find that they become enemies. When one defeats the other, the victor must, in turn, expect a third person to try to take away what he has won.

So it is clear what men are like when there is no outside power to keep them all in fear. Such a state of nature becomes a condition of war. In such a war, every man struggles with every other man. War does not only mean constant fighting. A period of time during which a willingness to fight is commonly known and accepted is also called war.

So in the state of nature, every man is every other man's enemy. There is no safety or security except one's own strength and trickery. In this state of things, there can be no factories or stores because products are always unsafe. There can be no farming, no trading, no large buildings, no arts, no sciences, no society. Worst of all there would be continual fear and danger of violent death. The life of man would be solitary, poor, nasty, brutish, and short.

This state of nature might not actually have existed, and I certainly do not believe it existed throughout the world. Yet if we look at what men are now like in societies, we can convince ourselves how men would be in a purely natural condition. At night we all lock our houses and when we walk the streets, we are constantly on guard. This shows that we believe that only fear of an outside power keeps men in check. Nations and kings who have nothing to fear act toward one another just as we describe individual men acting in a state of nature. When a peaceful society falls into civil war, we see what men are really like outside of society.

8

The Prince
Niccolò Machiavelli

I wish now to speak about how a ruler should treat his friends and subjects. Many famous authors have written about this, and I am afraid you will think that I am being arrogant for writing about it again. This is especially so since what I have to say is so different from what the famous authors of the past have said. They have written about imaginary governments that don't exist in reality. To me it seems more useful to write down the simple truth of the matter.

There is such a great difference between how human beings actually live and how they ought to live. A ruler who ignores what is being done by human beings in order to think about what ought to be done will bring about his own destruction. Since a ruler always has subjects who are not good, he too must learn how not to be good.

Let us therefore stop talking about imaginary things and start saying what is true about a ruler. All men, rulers included, are said to have qualities for which they are praised and blamed. Some men are called generous, others stingy, some cruel, others merciful, some treacherous, others faithful, some cowardly, others brave, some religious, others unreligious, and so on.

Everyone will agree that it would be nice if a ruler had all the qualities mentioned above that are considered good. However, it is impossible to have them all, for human nature is not like that. The ruler should be smart enough not to get the reputation for having those bad qualities which could cause him to lose power. As for the other bad qualities, he should not worry too much about his reputation. If he thinks about the matter carefully, he will see that if he tries to acquire certain qualities that seem good, he might lose his power. On the other hand, some other qualities that seem bad will help him increase his power.

Mathematical Principles
Sir Isaac Newton

Laws of Motion

Law A

A body that is either at rest or in motion with constant speed in a straight line stays that way. It changes its speed or direction only when forced to do so by something else.

If you throw something, it will keep on moving at constant speed in a straight line. However, all bodies are slowed down by air resistance or pulled downward by the force of gravity. A top would not stop spinning if it were not slowed down by moving through the air. Planets and comets are much bigger and move through space in which there is very little air resistance. They therefore keep their motions, both circular and in a straight line, for a much longer time.

Law B

To every action there is always an opposed and equal reaction. That is, when two bodies act on one another, these actions are equal but in opposite directions.

A body that pushes or pulls another body is pushed or pulled by that other just as much. If you press a stone with your finger, your finger is also pressed by the stone. If a horse pulls a stone tied to a rope, the horse (if I may say so) will be pulled back toward the stone just as much. This is because the rope that is being stretched pulls the horse toward the stone as much as the stone toward the horse.

10

The Confessions
Saint Augustine of Hippo

God, your law punishes theft. This law is written in our hearts, and no amount of evil or crime can erase it. We can see this because no thief, not even a rich one, will let another man, even one who is very poor, steal from him. Yet, I both wanted to steal and did steal. And what is so surprising, I was not forced to do it because I needed anything. I stole something that I already had. I stole pears, although I already had pears that were better than the ones I took. I had no wish to eat what I stole. What I enjoyed was stealing itself.

Near my parents' garden was a neighbor's pear tree. Although it was loaded with fruit, the pears looked rotten. Some friends and I got the idea of shaking the pears off the tree and carrying them away. We set out late at night and stole all the fruit we could carry. We tasted a few and then threw the rest to the pigs. The pleasure we felt was simply in doing something that was forbidden. We took no pleasure in eating the pears nor in being out late at night.

The Manual
Epictetus

Some things are in our power and control, while others aren't. It is in our power to decide what we think about things and to decide which things we are going to pursue. It is also in our power to decide what we like and don't like. In a word, we control our own actions. Outside our power and control are all bodies in the world, including even our own bodies and our own property. Also, we have no control over our reputations and no control over whether people listen to us or not. Again, in a word, what are not our own actions.

The things that are in our power are by nature free. Those that are not in our power are weak, slavish, and belong to others. Remember, then, if you start thinking that slavish things are free or that what belongs to others belongs to you, you will feel trapped. You will blame both gods and men. But if you suppose that what really belongs to you does belong to you and that what really belongs to another does belong to another, you will be free. No one will ever force you. No one can ever stop you. You won't ever blame anyone for anything. You'll do nothing against your own will. You will have no enemies, because no one will be able to hurt you.

If you decide to pursue such great things, you must also decide not to be attracted by money, property, reputation, and all the other things that are outside your control. You must give up some of them completely. The others you must postpone for the time being.

If you want to be free, to have no enemies, to do nothing against your will, and, at the same time, to rule and control others and be rich, you will surely fail. You can become free and happy only if you gain power and control over yourself.

12

Pensées
Blaise Pascal

Even as children we are told to take care of our reputations, our property, and our friends. We are even told to look after the reputations and property of our friends. We are given chores and homework and are constantly told that we will not be happy unless both we and our friends have health, good reputations, and money in the bank. If one thing goes wrong, we are told we will be unhappy. So, from the first moment of each day we are burdened with responsibilities.

You will say that this is a strange way to make people happy. Could one even imagine a better way to make them unhappy? But what should one do? If you took people's worries away they would be forced to look at themselves. They would have to think about what they are, where they come from, and where they are going. For many, these thoughts would be unbearable. This is why people have to keep busy. Even when they have free time, they are advised to spend it keeping busy with sports and hobbies. Isn't such a person's heart empty and ugly?

Introduction to Experimental Medicine
Claude Bernard

Do we have the right to experiment on animals? As for me, I think we definitely have this right. It would be strange if we said that human beings have the right to use animals for food, but don't have the right to use them for learning things that are useful for preserving human life. You cannot deny that progress in medicine requires experiments. We can save some living beings from death only by killing others. Experiments must be made, either on human beings or on animals. If it is wrong to do experiments on human beings, then it must be right to do experiments on animals. This is true even if the experiments are painful and dangerous to the animal, as long as they are useful to human beings.

What about the objections of some serious people who are not scientists? They feel that experiments on animals are wrong because the animals suffer. They think the scientists who do these experiments are cruel. But what about a soldier who has to kill for his country, or a surgeon who must hurt someone in order to cure him? Are they also cruel? Are they like a person who likes to hurt other people? I don't think so! What makes them different is the ideas they have. The doctor wants to cure disease. The soldier wants to protect his country. In the same way, the medical scientist who does experiments on living animals wants to learn things. He is following his own scientific idea. He doesn't hear the cries of the animals or see the blood that is flowing. What other people find disgusting, he finds interesting. As long as he is under the influence of the scientific idea, nothing else matters very much to him. People who don't share his idea will think that he is cruel, and he won't be able to convince them that he isn't. He will be able to discuss what he does only with other scientists. Only his own conscience can tell him whether what he is doing is right or wrong.

The Republic: The Ring of Gyges
Plato

Do people behave justly because they want to? Or are they just and fair because they are afraid to be unjust? To answer these questions, let us pretend we can give both the just and unjust man the freedom and power to do whatever he pleases. Then in our imaginations we can see where his desires will lead him. The just person will be no different from the unjust person. For he looks to what is to his self-interest just as much as the unjust man does. Only fear of the law makes him just. Let me tell you a story about a man who had such freedom.

People say that he was a shepherd in the service of the king of Lydia. After a great rainstorm and an earthquake, the ground opened up where he was caring for sheep, and he went into the opening in the earth. The story goes on to say that he saw many marvels there, among which was a hollow bronze horse with little doors. When he looked in, he saw the body of a giant with a gold ring on its hand. He took the ring and left.

When the shepherds held their monthly meeting to report to the king about his flocks, this shepherd also attended, wearing the ring. While he was sitting there twisting the ring on his finger, he happened to turn it so that the stone faced his palm. When he did this, the story goes on, he became invisible to those who sat around him. They spoke about him as if he were not there. He was amazed, and fumbled with his ring. When he turned the stone out, he became visible again. He tested this many times, and found that the ring really possessed this power of making him invisible when he wanted. So with the help of this ring, he seduced the king's wife, and got her to help him kill the king and take over his kingdom.

Now suppose we have two such rings. Let's give one to a just man and the other to an unjust man. It is hard to believe that even a just man would stop himself from stealing if he knew he would never get caught.

On Colliding Bodies
Christian Huygens

Hypothesis I: Any body already in motion continues to move forever with the same speed, and in a straight line, unless it is interfered with.

Hypothesis II: Let us suppose that two identical bodies traveling at the same speed collide with one another. After the collision, each rebounds with the same speed it had before the collision.

Hypothesis III: The speed of a body is always determined in relation to other bodies that we consider to be at rest. However, the body the speed of which we are trying to determine and the bodies that we consider to be at rest could all in addition have a common motion. Since this additional motion is common to all the bodies, it doesn't affect any of our conclusions. This means that if we allow two bodies to collide, and, in addition to their motion toward one another, they both share a common motion, the result is the same as if that common motion were totally absent.

15b

Mathematical Principles, Law A
Sir Isaac Newton

Law A

A body that is either at rest or in motion with constant speed in a straight line stays that way. It changes its speed or direction only when forced to do so by something else.

If you throw something, it will keep on moving at constant speed in a straight line. However, all bodies are slowed down by air resistance or pulled downward by the force of gravity. A top would not stop spinning if it were not slowed down by moving through the air. Planets and comets are much bigger and move through space in which there is very little air resistance. They therefore keep their motions, both circular and in a straight line, for a much longer time.

16

Passers-By
Franz Kafka

When you go walking at night up a street and a man, visible a long way off for the street goes uphill and there is a full moon comes running toward you, well, you don't catch hold of him as he passes. You let him run on even if he is a feeble old man, even if someone is chasing him and yelling at him.

For it is night, and you can't help it if the street goes uphill in the moonlight. And besides, these two have maybe started the chase to amuse themselves, or perhaps they are both chasing a third person, or perhaps the first is an innocent man and the second wants to murder him and so you would become an accessory, or they are merely running separately home to bed, or perhaps the first has a gun.

And anyhow, haven't you a right to be tired, haven't you been drinking a lot of wine? You're thankful they are now both long out of sight.

The Metaphysics
Aristotle

All human beings naturally want to know. A sign of this is that we like to use our senses: to see and hear and smell and touch and taste. We like to use our senses even when we are not using them to do something else. But, most of all, we like to see. Even when there is nothing we plan to do, we enjoy seeing almost more than anything else. This is because seeing, most of all, makes us know that one thing differs from another and that things have parts.

All animals are born with the ability to sense. In addition to this, some kinds of animals are able to remember. Other kinds are not able to remember. The ones that are able to remember are also able to learn.

So some animals live by sense experience and memory, but have only a small share in what we call real experience. Only the human animal has real experience, since only human beings are able to make many memories into one connected experience. There is what we might call experience or skill or know-how, and there is also what we might call art or knowledge. Experience makes us know that when Mary had this illness and when John had that illness, the same kind of treatment cured both of them. But only art or knowledge makes us know generally that anybody with an illness of a certain kind can be cured by a certain kind of treatment. Art and knowledge are impossible without experience. But art and knowledge make us know more than experience does. They make us know about relations among kinds of things or classes of things. Experience only teaches about relations between particular things.

Another way of stating this difference is to say that, in experience, we do not know causes, while through art and knowledge, we do know causes. So there is sensing, then remembering, then having a connected experience, and then having art and knowledge. When we have art and knowledge, we know about kinds of things and about causes.

The Elements
Euclid

Proposition I

On a given straight line to construct a triangle
with all the sides equal to one another.

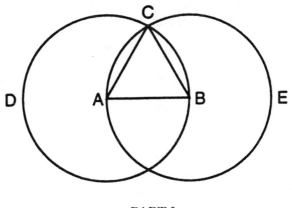

PART I

Let *AB* be the given straight line. We wish to construct an equilateral triangle on *AB*. Draw circle *DCB* with center *A* and radius *AB*. Again, with center *B* and radius *BA*, let circle *ACE* be drawn. From point *C* where the circles cut one another, draw straight lines *AC* and *BC* to the points *A* and *B*.

PART II

Now, since point A is the center of the circle DCB, AC is equal to AB. This is because on a circle, all points are the same distance from the center. Again, since point B is the center of the circle ACE, BC is equal to AB. But AC was also proved equal to AB. Therefore each of the straight lines AC and BC is equal to AB.

PART III

Since things that are equal to the same thing are equal to each other, AC is also equal to BC. The three lines AC, AB, and BC are therefore equal to one another. But these three lines form a triangle. Therefore, the triangle ABC has three equal sides, that is, is equilateral, and has been constructed on the line AB. That is what was to be done.

19

The Seven Books
Mencius

I

Mencius went to see King Hwuy of Leang. "Honored sir," the king said to Mencius. "Since you have not considered it too far to travel here, though it is a distance of over a thousand miles, may I presume to ask if you have advice that can profit my kingdom?"

Mencius replied, "Why must Your Majesty use that word *profit*? I do indeed have advice, but it is always about righteousness and benevolence. If Your Majesty says, 'What can profit my kingdom?' the generals and high officials will say, 'What can profit our families?' The lower officials and the common people will ask, 'How can we profit ourselves?' Everyone will try to seize this profit, and the kingdom will be threatened. If righteousness is put last and profit first, then no one will be satisfied without seizing everything. There has never been a man trained to righteousness who didn't think first of his sovereign. Let Your Majesty say, 'Benevolence and righteousness shall be our only themes.' Why must you use that word *profit*?"

II

Mencius said, "Men's minds cannot bear to see the sufferings of others. My meaning can be illustrated by this example. Even in these days, if we suddenly see a child about to fall into a well, we all experience a feeling of alarm and distress. We do not feel this way because we want the favor of the child's parents or the praise of our friends and neighbors. Nor do we feel this way because we are afraid of getting a reputation for callousness. We simply feel distressed when we see a child about to be injured.

"From this example, we can recognize that without a feeling for the misery and suffering of another, we would not be human. Nor would we be human if we didn't feel shame for our own lack of goodness, and anger and distaste at its absence in others. No less important to what we are is our feeling of modesty. In modesty, we separate ourselves from our own concerns and desires, and recognize the concerns and desires in others. The last feeling that makes us human is our approval of what is good and our disapproval of what isn't. The feeling for another's misery is the principle of benevolence. The feeling of shame and anger is the principle of righteousness. The feeling of modesty is the principle of propriety or of what is one's own. The feeling of approval and disapproval is the principle of knowledge."

III

Mencius said, "If someone loves others, and others do not love him in return, let him turn inward and examine his own benevolence. If someone tries to rule others and his rule is unsuccessful, let him turn inward and examine his own wisdom. If he treats others politely and they do not return his politeness, let him turn inward and examine his own feeling of respect. When, by our efforts, we do not achieve what we desire, we must turn inward and examine ourselves in what we do. When someone really acts correctly, the whole empire turns to him with recognition and submission."

IV

Mencius said, "What distinguishes a superior man from others is what he holds in his heart; namely, benevolence and propriety. The benevolent man loves others. The man of propriety shows others respect. He who loves others is loved by them. He who respects others is always respected by them.

"What if we meet a man who treats us in a perverse and unreasonable way? In such a situation, the superior man will first turn around upon himself. He will say to himself, 'I must have been lacking in benevolence; I must have been lacking in propriety. How did this happen in me?' He examines himself and is especially benevolent. He turns around on himself and is especially observant of propriety. However, what if the other's perversity and unreasonableness remain the same? The superior man will again turn around on himself and say, 'I must have been failing to do my utmost.' He again turns on himself and makes even greater exertions. However, the perversity and unreasonableness may well continue. If they do, the superior man now says, 'This man is utterly lost. Since he acts in this way, he is no different from an animal, and why should I struggle with an animal?'"

The Confessions
Saint Augustine of Hippo

Music holds an important place in my heart. Yet sometimes it seems to me that I give it more importance than is right. I know that when holy words are sung well, our minds are stirred up to a burning religious feeling. We then experience a much deeper flame of devotion than when these words are just spoken. However, our emotions are of many different kinds. By some secret link, each emotion is stirred up by a certain type of song. Often I'm tricked by this fact. I received pleasure from holy songs, which my mind or soul should not feel. In church we should only feel the pleasures that our reason allows. Unfortunately, instead of following behind reason, our desire for pleasure often tries to take the lead. In the case of holy music, I sin without realizing it. After the singing has stopped, I often recognize that it was my body and not my soul that was pleased.

When I worry about being tricked in this way, I fall into the error of being too strict. At those times, I want all music banished from the church. The safer course, then, appears to be what a famous bishop of Alexandria once suggested. A reader of Psalms, he said, should use so little change of voice that the effort is more like speaking than singing. But then I remember the tears I used to shed in church when Psalms were sung. This was just at the time when I was beginning to recover my faith. And I know that now I am often moved by the words sung and not by the singing. Once again, I see how important music can be. So I am sometimes convinced by the danger of the pleasure, and other times persuaded by the good that can be done. On the whole, I am inclined to favor singing in church. My hope is that the delight in pleasing sounds will stir weaker minds to a feeling of devotion. Yet for me, even now, the danger is still there. Whenever I am more moved by the singing than by the words, I think it would be better for me not to hear the music.

The Will to Believe
William James

A religious person believes that the more perfect and more eternal aspect of the universe has a personal form. Religions call this aspect, or part, "God." A religious person cannot believe that the entire universe is a mere thing. Rather, part of the universe is a sort of person, a "Thou," God. Furthermore, religions hold that any relation that may be possible from person to person might also be possible here. We all recognize that we are in part passive portions of the universe and that some things just happen to us. However, we also believe that we ourselves can take the first step and do things. This belief leads to the possibility that religion asks us to use our ability to take the first step. It might be that evidence for religious beliefs is withheld unless we meet it halfway.

Let me give an example. Imagine a person who was in the habit of going to the same club everyday. While there, he never greeted anyone first. Whenever anyone told him something, he never believed it without proof. He even went so far as to ask for everything in writing. How would other people respond to him? Don't you think that he would miss out on the pleasures of friendship he would have had if he had been more trusting? I believe that the universe might be like that. If we go around always asking for proof of God's existence, we might never get to know him at all if he exists. To get any evidence at all of God's existence, we might have to take the first step.

The Peloponnesian Wars
Thucydides

Athens and Sparta, the two most powerful cities in Greece, had been at war with one another for many years. Athens, a great naval power, controlled most of the islands in the Aegean Sea. It was creating an empire, but some of the islands were not eager to join. One such island was Melos, which had been colonized by Sparta and wished to remain neutral. In the 16th year of the war, an Athenian fleet sailed to the island of Melos. As soon as the Athenian army landed, they sent ambassadors to negotiate with the most important men on the island.

ATHENIANS: We don't plan to pretend we have a right to be on your island. In return, don't you bother telling us you won't join our enemies, the Spartans, or that you've never hurt us. All these claims would only hide the real issue. We both know the way the world is. Right and wrong come into play only between people whose power is equal. Otherwise, the strong do what they can. The weak suffer whatever is necessary.

MELIANS: You tell us to forget what is right and only consider what is in our self-interest. Agreed! Even so, it couldn't be useful to anyone—us or you—to deny us a privilege always allowed those in great danger. When someone is threatened, he is permitted to bring up what is fair and right. At those times, one is even allowed to use arguments that aren't quite logical if he can get them accepted. You Athenians should want to protect this custom too. You'll need it if you're ever defeated. For people will avenge themselves on you.

ATHENIANS: We're not afraid of the end of our empire. What is worse is subjects who attack and overpower their rulers. We're here, therefore, for the present interests of our empire. We want to rule you for the good of us both.

MELIANS: We'd love to hear how it's as good for us to serve you as for you to rule us.

ATHENIANS: You would gain by not being destroyed. We would gain by not destroying you.

MELIANS: So we can't be neutral.

ATHENIANS: No. Your hostility can't hurt us much. But to our subjects, your neutrality may look like our weakness.

MELIANS: But we're not in the same category as your subjects. They are either your colonists or those who have rebelled against you. We're neither.

ATHENIANS: To our subjects, there are only two kinds of people. There are those we rule and those we don't rule. And our subjects believe if we don't rule a people, it is because they're strong. If we don't attack them, it is because we are afraid. You're weaker than many of our subjects. We can't let you escape the masters of the sea.

MELIANS: All right. You won't let us talk about justice. We'll talk about self-interest. Our interests and yours are the same. Many cities and islands are still neutral. If you attack us, they'll think they're next. So they'll become your enemies even though they wouldn't have thought of doing so.

ATHENIANS: Neutrals on land don't concern us. It's the islanders like you and our discontented subjects who worry us. Both could take rash steps and lead themselves and us into danger.

MELIANS: If your subjects will risk so much to be free of you, how can you expect us to submit to you? We're still free. Shouldn't we try everything to avoid losing that?

ATHENIANS: If honor and shame were at stake, then perhaps you should. But they're not an issue because we're so much stronger than you. All you have to worry about is simply how to preserve yourselves.

MELIANS: Anything can happen in war. Numbers aren't always the crucial thing. If we fight, there's still a chance.

ATHENIANS: Hope is very dangerous. Only those who have something to spare, something extra, can afford to hope. Hope can tempt us to absurd actions. We only recognize how flimsy our hope was when we are ruined. You are weak. Your survival hangs on a single throw of the dice. You can't risk hope. That's the way to destruction.

MELIANS: We know you are stronger. But we trust in the help of the gods since we are just men fighting against unjust men.

ATHENIANS: We have gods too. And there is a law that gods and men rule wherever they can. We didn't create this law. It was here before us. It will still exist after us. We act by it knowing that you, having our power, would do the same.

The Melians and Athenians then went to war. After a hard fight, Athens won. The Athenians killed all the Melian men. They sold the women and children into slavery.

23

Introduction to Leadership Roles

Note: This material is included for reference only. You will be able to record your answers on the worksheet for the lesson.

What Should a Touchstones Discussion Leader Do?

Listed below are 10 situations in which a Touchstones Discussion leader must make a decision about what to do. Three possible actions are given for each situation. For each situation, circle the intervention you would choose as the discussion leader.

1. If there is a five-second period of silence, I would
   a. ask another question;
   b. call on a student to speak; or
   c. wait a little longer to see whether a student will speak.

2. If the group strays very far from the text, I would
   a. bring the class back to the text;
   b. allow the discussion to continue if many students are participating in it; or
   c. ask the students whether they think they are talking about the reading.

3. If some members of the group keep talking to their neighbors, I would
   a. tell them to stop and remind them of the ground rules;
   b. ask them whether they would like to say what they just said to the whole group; or
   c. pretend not to notice it.

4. If a few students always do most of the talking, I would
   a. keep the group divided into small groups for most of the next two classes;
   b. speak to the students outside of class and let them know they are making it difficult for others to speak; or
   c. allow the whole class to discuss how the discussion can be improved.

5. If a few students always get into arguments with one another, I would
   a. find a way for these students to cooperate with one another by giving them joint responsibility for some class activity;
   b. point it out to them the next time they start to argue; or
   c. select other students as observers for a discussion and hope they report on it during the discussion about group dynamics.

6. If a few students make it impossible for there to be any discussion at all, I would
   a. remove them from the class;
   b. make them observers; or
   c. let the whole group discuss the situation.

7. If there is a 15-second period of silence, I would
   a. ask another question;
   b. call on a student to speak; or
   c. wait a little longer to see whether a student will speak.

8. If some students are always silent, I would
   a. observe whether they participate during small group work, and if they do, not worry;
   b. speak to the students outside of class to find out how to make it easier for them to speak;
   c. remember what they bring up in their opening questions. If the discussion is ever about that question, I would mention that fact during class and ask those individuals their thoughts.

9. If some students always interrupt or refuse to listen to certain other students, I would
   a. put these students together for small group work;
   b. point out the general problem to the class without mentioning names and ask how the whole class could improve the situation; or
   c. ask a few other students to act as observers and bring this up in the discussion on discussion.

10. If some students are interested in certain texts and not in others, I would
   a. explain that what makes a discussion interesting is not the text but what the students bring to it;
   b. let the group members talk about why they are interested in some texts and not in others; or
   c. assume this feeling will pass when the students have more experience, and I would not bring it up.

Student Leadership Guide

You, a few of your classmates, and your teacher will conduct an upcoming discussion class. A text has already been chosen for your class and now you must decide which of the activities listed below you will use. Although the lesson plan has already been written for you, feel free to modify it on the basis of your answers to the following questions.

1. Should the students write out their opening questions?

2. Should the students do small group work?

3. What should they work on in small groups?

4. Should each student leader be a member of a small group?

5. Before a question is asked to start discussion in the large group, should each student read a possible opening question?

6. Should all the students be participants or should some act as observers? If some are to be observers, should they fill out the observation sheets, draw maps of who speaks to whom, or do something else? Should there be just a few observers or as many as half the group? Should the observers and participants switch roles? Should they report to the group after the discussion?

7. Should there be a discussion about the discussion? If so, should this happen in the large group or in the small groups?

The Ethics
Aristotle

A man is thought to be great who thinks that he is worthy of great things, and is worthy of them. If a man thinks that he is worthy of great things but is not, then he is only a fool. Self-esteem is connected to greatness, and a great person knows he deserves to be honored by others.

A truly great man must be the best in every way. For example, it would be wrong for a great man to run from danger, or to do wrong to someone else.

The great man is mostly concerned with honors, but only if they are given by good men. He will despise honors given by men who are less good or even bad, and honors given for petty reasons. He will not care much about wealth and power, and he won't be overjoyed at good luck, or depressed if things go bad. So you can see why great men are thought to be proud. But some men are proud without having a right to be. They are only imitating what great men are, but are not themselves really great.

The great man likes to give favors, but he is ashamed of receiving them. To give is the mark of a superior person, and to have a favor done to you is to be inferior. The great man will forget or ignore favors done to him, but will remember those he does for others.

The great man won't do many things, because not very many things are worthy of him. But the things he does, he will do excellently, and they will be great things. He will never do anything secretly, nor hide his true feelings. This is what cowards do. So he always tells the truth. He has very few friends. Friends should be equals, and very few people are his equals. He doesn't praise or blame people. He would only praise people and their acts if they were better than him or his acts. On the other hand, he expects everyone else to behave worse, so why blame them?

Finally, a great man will walk slowly and speak evenly and in a low tone, for to walk quickly and speak fast and in a high tone is a sign that you are excited and out of control. A great man thinks there is nothing worth getting excited and worried about.

Such, then, is the great man.

24

25

The Assayer
Galileo

I cannot imagine a body that doesn't have a definite size and shape. I must also imagine it being in a particular place at some particular time. This body must either be in motion or at rest. It is either in contact with some other body, or alone. No matter how hard I try, I cannot separate my idea of a body from these conditions. However, I don't think the same is true of colors, tastes, sounds, and smells. I think that colors, tastes, sounds, and smells don't belong to the body at all, but are only in the eyes, tongue, ears, and nose of whoever observes the body. The observer could be a human being or some other animal. If there were no animals in the world, there wouldn't be colors, tastes, sounds, and smells. Yet, we ordinarily believe that these belong to a body as much as shape, size, position, time, and motion do. For example, don't we ordinarily believe that the color of a table belongs to it as much as its shape does? I think this is wrong.

I think I can explain what I mean better if I give an example. Suppose I move my hand first over a marble statue of a man and then over a living man. In both cases, I am doing the same thing with my hand. I am moving my hand and touching the bodies at the same time. But when I touch the living man on the soles of his feet, he says he is being tickled. Would you want to say that the hand had in itself the property of tickling? When I move my hand over the statue, it surely isn't being tickled. Tickling belongs entirely to a living and sensing animal. If there were no animals in the world, there would be no tickling. I believe the same is true about colors, tastes, sounds, and smells.

26

The Iliad: Achilles and Priam
Homer

In the 10th year of the war between the Greeks and the Trojans, the greatest Greek warrior, Achilles, killed the most courageous and strongest Trojan, Hector. Because Hector had killed Achilles' closest friend, the Greek was not satisfied by his enemy's death. For days, Achilles insulted Hector's dead body as the Trojan's father, King Priam, longing to recover his son's body for burial, remained helpless in his city. Each day, Achilles dragged Hector's dead body through the dust. At night he returned to his tent to rest, refusing to eat. This day was no different. He rested in his tent waiting for the dawn when he would continue his revenge against the dead man.

Suddenly Achilles saw a tall kingly old man before him. It was Priam, king of the Trojans, and father of Hector. Priam kneeled before the Greek and kissed the hands that had killed so many of his sons. "Achilles, remember your own father," Priam said. "He must be my age. Perhaps right now in a faraway country, people are causing him pain. But nothing he suffers can compare with my misery. He is happy knowing that you, his son, are still alive. I once had 50 sons, but now most are dead. Yet worst of all is the death of my best son, Hector. You killed him, and now I come all alone into your camp to ask for his body. Take pity on me. Remember your own father. For I am more to be pitied than any man alive. What other man has had to come through great danger to kiss the hand of his son's killer?"

Priam's words stirred in Achilles a great sadness for his own father. He pushed the old man's hands away gently. Priam sat on the floor. Achilles remained on the stool. They sat near one another, each remembering those who were not there. Priam wept for his dead son, Hector. Achilles, looking at Priam' face, wept for his own absent father and for his dead friend. The young warrior and the old king wept together.

When the Greek had had enough of his grief, he got up from his chair. He took the old king's hand and raised him to his feet. "How could you have risked coming to my ships, old man? Your heart must be iron. Sit on this chair and you and I will end our grief. What's the use of weeping? We both know what everyone's life is like. The god, Zeus, has two jars. One holds good things, the other contains troubles and misery. Each person gets some of both. Sometimes one has good fortune. Other times one has bad fortune. This is how it was for my own father. He was a ruler of men, had riches and property and was given a goddess for a wife. Yet, he, too, received evil. Unlike you, he had only one son and I give him no help as he grows old. I sit here, far away, bringing pain and sorrow to you and your children. And you, Priam once ruled this whole area with your sons. Now your kingdom must fight constantly, and your sons are dead. Don't mourn endlessly. You can never bring Hector back to life."

"Achilles," said the old king, "don't make me sit here while my dead son still lies in the dust. Please let me see him and take him home. The presents I've brought are valuable. Take them and give me my son."

Achilles frowned and stared at Priam. "Don't stir me up, old man! I give him back because I give him back. Don't remind me of my own grief or I may strike you even here in my tent."

Priam was frightened. The young Greek warrior, moving like a lion, left the tent. He took the ransom out of Priam's wagon and then went to find serving-maids. He ordered them to wash Hector's dead body. He did this because he was afraid Priam would break down at the sight of his son's dirty, broken body. The old man might be unable to hold back his anger. Achilles was afraid that this would remind him of his own grief and he would, there in his tent, kill the old man.

Achilles returned to his tent and spoke. "Priam, we must both eat. Even Niobe, whose 12 children were killed, ate when she was worn out with crying. Afterwards you can take your son home to bury him."

The two men ate. These two men, who had wept and mourned together, now looked at one another. Each admired the other. Achilles appeared as a god to the old king. Priam appeared brave and dignified to the young warrior. The two men then slept. At dawn, Priam put his son on the wagon and took him home to bury him and to prepare his people to fight again.

Second Treatise of Civil Government
John Locke

How could anyone ever come to own anything, that is, to have property? This question appears a great difficulty to some writers. I, however, will try to show that property can emerge out of what God gave everyone in common. In fact, I will show that this even occurred without any written or spoken agreement among people.

God gave the world to all people in common. He has also given us reason and thought to make use of the things in the world to stay alive and even improve our lives. The earth and everything on it were first given to us for our support and comfort. All the fruits it naturally produces and the animals it feeds belonged to everyone in common. No one had a private rule or right over anything in the original natural state of human beings. Yet, fruits and animals are on the earth for our use. There must therefore be a way that a particular person can rightly acquire some fruit or animals in order actually to use them for his benefit. The fruit or meat that a wild Indian eats must first become his possession so that others no longer have a right to it. Otherwise, how can it do him any good for keeping himself alive? If there is no way for him rightfully to eat fruit, then eating fruit would always mean stealing it from everyone else.

By nature, the earth and all the lower animals are the common possession of everyone. However, each person owns himself. No one has a right to his person but himself. The labor of his body and the work of his hands are therefore also properly his. Whatever he himself removes from nature has thereby been mixed with which was already his own and made what he removed his property. By his labor, he has joined to the fruit something that excludes everyone else. A person's labor is without any question his own property. No one but he can have a right to what it is joined to. This is true at least where there is still enough fruit left for others to use.

A person who picks apples from a tree in the woods that no one owns and eats them has certainly made them his own. The nourishment is his. I ask, when did the apples begin to be his? When he ate them or digested them or when he brought them home? It's plain that if the first gathering of the apples didn't make them his, nothing else could. His labor made those apples different from all others. He added to those apples something more than nature had done. They then became his private property.

28

The Metaphysics of Morals
Immanuel Kant

When we can, we should give to others who are in need. It's one of our duties. We also know there are many people who give because they enjoy giving and not because it's a duty. They are pleased when they can give to others. They act without any hidden purpose such as self-interest or because they want to feel important. They are just kind, decent people. I claim there is a great difference between kind people and those who give because it's their duty. Giving because it's our duty has moral value. The same action, when done simply from kindness, has no moral worth at all. When a kind person helps another, he is only doing what he wants to do. In this action, he is no different from anyone doing what he wants.

Suppose we very much want to honor someone. If it turns out to be useful to the public and in agreement with duty, it is perfectly fine to do it. Our action should be praised and encouraged. But we shouldn't be esteemed or admired for what we did. Our action lacked a real moral support. The support for our action should have been our duty, whether we felt like honoring that person or not. In the example we just gave, we wanted to honor someone. It just turned out to have been the right thing to do.

Take the case of a philanthropist, someone who loves others and gives money, food, or buildings to people he doesn't even know. Suppose that he feels great sorrow because of a personal loss. He no longer cares about the troubles of others because now he is so overwhelmed by his own. Yet, he is still rich and powerful enough to help others who need it. Suppose now that he tears himself away from his own pain. He gives money to others because it is his duty and not only, as in the past, because he wanted to. Then, for the first time, his action will have real moral worth.

Take another example. Suppose there is a decent person who is cold-hearted and indifferent to the suffering and pain of others. Suppose also that he is very patient when he suffers. In addition, he also expects that other people should be just like him in difficult times. Such a person would not be the worst creature produced by nature. But even though he is not the sort of person who naturally loves and cares for others, he would still have in himself something far better than natural kindness. Would he not have a source of action that would give him a worth far greater than what comes from being good-natured and kind? Yes, without any doubt! Every person, whatever that person is like, can possess a moral worth that is, without any comparison, the greatest possible. In the cases we have looked at, such a person can be loving and caring and generous toward others from duty rather than because he wants by natural feeling to be that way.

The Origin of Species
Charles Darwin

It has been said that all animals, and even plants, must struggle with one another in order to live. Nothing is easier than to
admit this in words. Nothing is harder than to keep it constantly in mind. Yet, if we don't keep it in mind, we will misunder-
stand most of the things we see when we look at nature. At first
glance, the face of nature is bright with gladness. We forget that
the birds that are singing around us live on insects and seeds.
They are constantly destroying life. We also forget that these
birds and their eggs are themselves being destroyed by other
birds and animals. One year there seems to be plenty of food.
The next year there is starvation.

People have said that connections of all the living beings on
earth to one another can be represented by a great tree. Let us
consider the relation between this peaceful-looking tree and the
struggle for life. The green and budding twigs represent the
kinds of living things we see around us now. The green and budding twigs from previous years represent those kinds of animals
and plants, like the saber-toothed tiger, which used to exist and
don't any more. All the growing twigs compete with one another for light just as kinds of animals compete with one another in
the great battle for life. The big branches of the tree that were

once small budding twigs now give rise to other branches. In the same way, animals that once lived and roamed the earth, and do so no more, have given rise to others until we come to the animals living today.

Of the many twigs that grew when the tree was small, only two or three survive. These are the biggest branches of the tree. From them all the other branches arise. So it is with animals that lived long ago. Very few of them have living descendants. They are known to us only from their bones that are buried in the earth. The buds on the tree give rise to other buds and the stronger branches cut off the light from the weaker ones and kill them. This is the great struggle for life in which only the strong survive and the weak perish. In the same way, the Great Tree of Life fills the earth with its dead and broken branches and covers its surface with beautiful green buds.

The Republic: The Image of the Cave
Plato

Socrates is speaking with his young friend, Glaucon.

SOCRATES: Glaucon, let's try to think about what human life is like ordinarily, and what it might be like for someone who somehow got to know the truth about it. Imagine that all human beings live in a cave under the earth. The cave has an entrance open to the light of day. But the human beings are chained so that they can neither move, nor turn toward the opening, nor even turn toward each other. They have been chained in this way since their childhood. Imagine also that there is a fire burning and glowing within the cave. It is above and behind the prisoners, casting shadows on the wall in front of them. They cannot see the fire. All the prisoners can see are shadows of themselves and of each other on the wall. They also see shadows cast by anything that is carried behind their backs between the glowing fire and themselves.

GLAUCON: This is a strange image, Socrates, and the prisoners are strange prisoners.

SOCRATES: In many ways, these prisoners are just like us. Do you think these people will see anything of themselves or each other except the shadows cast on the wall?

GLAUCON: No, not if they are not able to look in any direction except straight ahead.

SOCRATES: And what about the things carried past them, behind their backs? Would they see those things themselves, or only their shadows? Even worse, could they even know if they were missing something?

GLAUCON: No, perhaps they could not tell the difference.

SOCRATES: Would their conversations with each other be about anything real? Wouldn't they think that the shadows were real things?

GLAUCON: Yes, of course.

SOCRATES: Could these people ever be freed and healed of their ignorance?

GLAUCON: I don't know.

SOCRATES: What if something like this happened? I'm not sure how it would happen. Suppose one prisoner were freed from his chains, and forced suddenly to stand up, to turn around, to look, and to try to walk. Wouldn't he be confused and fright-ened when he saw the glow of the fire and when he saw the objects that cast the shadows he had been looking at before? But, what if he were forced to go on? Suppose he were dragged out into the light of day. Wouldn't he be frightened and confused again, as he saw the things that exist in the light of day, in the light of the sun? All he had seen before were shadows of things by firelight. Now he has to look upon things in the sun. At first, he couldn't look directly at these things, but, he could look at their shadows and at their reflections in ponds. After a while, he could look directly at the things in the light of the sun. Finally, after much difficulty, he would be able to look with gladness upon the sun itself.

How might the person who had gone through this journey think about where he had been before, and where he was now? I guess that the first part of his life might not seem so important anymore. His recent discoveries might seem like the most important things in the world. Also, after he thought about it, he might suspect that his fellow prisoners would not be glad to see him again, especially if they thought he knew something they didn't. They would especially resent him if he told them that the things they have spent their lives getting good at are unreal and unimportant. They might laugh at him because he was no longer good at dealing with things in the cave. Finally, they might even act from their resentment and try to kill him. Still, down again he must go, since he knows he has something good to offer his fellow prisoners, and he must try to learn how to do that as well as he can.

GLAUCON: If human life really is like life in the cave, then I can see why it would be dangerous for someone who had learned the truth about things to try to return to help those still there.

Printed in the United States
65239LVS00002B/1-12

9 781878 461391